TO MY BELOVED MOTHER

1932-2021

Artwork by: *Frances Jean Hamby Baugus*

WORKBOOK PRESS LLC
187 E Warm Springs Rd,
Suite B285, Las Vegas, NV 89119, USA

Website:	https://workbookpress.com/
Hotline:	1-888-818-4856
Email:	admin@workbookpress.com

Also Published by:
L. A. Espriux
Website:	WWW. ESPRIUX.COM
Email:	lespriux@outlook.com/ espriux@gmail.com
Facebook:	LA Espriux

Ordering Information:
Quantity sales. Special discounts are available on quantity purchases by corporations, associations, and others.
For details, contact the publishers at the address above.

Library of Congress Control Number:

| ISBN-13: | 000-0-000000-00-0 (Paperback Version) |
| | 000-0-000000-00-0 (Digital Version) |

REV. DATE: 05/27/2022

Where Water Goes Volume 1

Book of Parables

First Book of Parables

Bronzed-winged
the poet looks up
into sky deep
almost to touch stars
with readied pen

To see
shadow-dreams falling
as earth-bound
visions of snow geese
bones too heavy
to ascend the clouds

Below
night darker than night
made light by new wings
It is a soul changed beautiful
in an instant
soaring free into heaven
not alone

So begins the
First Book of Parables
before beginning
of this poem
to end

L. A. Espriux

WHERE WATER GOES

Where begins the water flow
From icy peaks a melting knoll
Along sheer steps of canyon walls
Tolls a river through ancient deeps
Restless traveler that never sleeps
All made whole by drips and drops
All one body that never stops
Tides that erase rich centuries spun
Rim of destiny reshaped beyond
Fire and ice to all in all suffice
To feed the world with promises and rice
And water flows where no one knows
Life and particle where wind blows
Where flesh wanders the spirit goes

L. A. Espriux

TRAVELED DISTANCE

Hearts broken yet to mend
Rich and beautiful places I have already been
Where sunsets golden splash a striated sky
Where dreams and shadows twined together lie
And I in ocean deep wish to sleep
Among the souls of noble men
To know no more the world of air and fire
To be free of love and all desire
And pass through the center to see the end
Atoms and constellations before times begin
Where galaxies adorn a celestial queen
From inside black holes chorus of angels sing
Where particles inferno of sun and wind
A spark of new heaven in me born again
Made of greater stuff than flesh and bone
A new star born bright in the night
A crystal light to see or to blind the sight
Distant traveler this world made to walk
Once to know as I am known

L. A. Espriux

Song of the Muse

There is the wind
Whispers desert time
Or is this rhythm of another rhyme
Circles height of sleepy trees
Saying softly
Saying sweet
Nothing is yours
Nothing to keep
I am free I am free
Come if you can
And catch me

There is the ocean
Licks sensual shore
Or is she something more
Slipping over silver sand
Saying softly
Saying sweet
Nothing is yours
Nothing to keep
I am free I am free
Come if you can
And catch me

There is the moon
Suspends silver thread
Or is his a crown of elusive head
Guardian over the fields of night
Saying softly
Saying sweet

Nothing is yours
Nothing to keep
I am free I am free
Come if you can
And catch me

In one voice sing the stars
I am me I am me
Come catch if you can
The myriad of the sand
Ride wind of the setting sun
Through course of light all must run
Into celestial valleys beyond mountains high
Zodiac maps drawn where constellations divide
Chase shadow of the moon
Into zenith of shadows noon

This poem made of things visible to see
Shaped by forces invisible that be

L. A. Espriux

REMEMBERING SHANGRI-LA

I remember that country
deep emperor green
as Shangri-La
In morning
dipped with silver dew
of fishermen songs
their nets tangled in twilight red
between humped gray shoals

I remember the women
black hair laced with flowers
exotic eyes deep fountains
reflecting the myriad night
of an east Asian hemisphere
How soft their touch
Their lips as fresh fruit
in a season golden with peace
Their laughter that fades
as morning in spring
as birds scattered
by a hunter's gun

I remember the silence before thunder
as orange flames spread rich
blistering the jungle fuse
Ghost of children wailing
in a smoky dawn mist
heavy with the dew
of burnt flesh
And all that remains black

twisted and scared
A rain of smoldering white ash
that has lasted and lasted
in my mind
to this day

L.A. Espriux

EMPEROR'S DREAM

The emperor
mounts pinnacle of an empire high
Sits he upon broken shoals of time
lattice of stars traversing sky
a narrow passage his reason to climb
eternity forever a distant soul to find
Clouded vision to judge the blind
above frozen peaks of younger rhyme
Before born emperor trapped in mortal lie

L. A. Espriux

MORE THAN THIS

I am not comely
as birds that sing
outside my window.

Nor am I strong
as hills of memory
jaded with rich promise.

I am not persistent
as relentless wind
to erase mountains soon.

Nor am I profound
as myriad of stars
reflecting eternity invisible.

But more than this I am
Made clay the image of man
Purposely designed by immortal hand.

L. A. Espriux

SMOKE IN THE AIR

smoke in the air
husk of a discarded cigarette within
silent depth of an onyx pool
the light fading softly
in her once lovely eyes
deep in reflection
a spirit-white ash
melted in time

smoke in the air
husk of a discarded cigarette
within silent grain of polished wood
a ribbon of death coiled
in her once lovely eyes
deep in reflection
a spirit-white ash
melted in time

L. A. Espriux

CHANGELING

I drink again
from the same mortal cup:
The same poison coursing my veins;
The same melancholy...
The same dying...

But now I live!
I who am born a brute!
I who walk fearless of all!
All that stand mortal against God!
I fear no shadow of living!
I fear no buried past!
Today I am tomorrow!

Yes--it is good to live again!
Yes--it is good my peace disturbed!
I pound my fi st against frozen silence!
Roll back the stone of all jealousy!
Now I remember the taste of blood!
The wolf-howl of wild men!
Me leader of the pack!

And only the moon moves complacent;
Moves naked among his consort of stars
unfettered that a beast risen from darkness
panting with rage in fields
below...

L. A. Espriux

EPITAPH

A man born in the hope of a lie
That his kingdom a place here on earth
Built by will and sweat of his brow
Until one day he sees his true refection
An image made weak and mortal now
Silently whispered in a chorus long ago

Loves lost in empty skies
Crosses in his heart till he dies
Tangled in shadows of his lies

A man snared in acts of twilight
His memories past remembering now
His dreams a dream of someone else
His once grand presence changed sifting sand
Forged of things dead but not buried
Silently whispered in a chorus long ago

Loves lost in empty skies
Crosses in his heart till he dies
Tangled in shadows of his lies

A man buried alive in many thoughts
All that he has planted seedless now
A beautiful wife mother to a child
Faded in visions no longer his desire
Only the haunting sound of her voice
Silently whispered in a chorus long ago

Loves lost in empty skies
Crosses in his heart till he dies
Tangled in shadows of his lies

A man forgotten in shade
His bones pressed back to earth at last
Past pleasure past pain past fear past love
His name forgotten and heartless now
His name recited on cold stone in a cemetery
Silently whispered in a chorus long ago

Loves lost to empty skies
Crosses in his heart till he dies
Tangled in shadows of his lies

L.A. Espriux

TRAFFIC INCIDENT

Wave of cars
at rush traffic
like an ocean roar
deafening and incessant
crash of nerves
slapping against steel and mortar
Dark smell of rubber
screams and squeals
squawks and knocks
mile piled upon mile
ebbing into a tide
of weeks and months and years

Then one evening before sunset
he has a revelation
Clarity of thought as never before
crawls free
from his stalled vehicle
his eyes transfixed heavenward
and pulls a revolver to his head

L.A. Espriux

Self Portrait

I glimpse my life today
reflected in a mirror
cracked and aged
as the portrait of Dorian Gray
cursed by an artist stroke

And I realize perplexedly
that I no longer see anything
and have grown sightless to the truth
trapped in mirror reflection
hidden in a corner
of life's truer self

Today an image
clear in the glass
a self faded and old
scarred with visions and dreams
and a body made of sand
circled as a snake
devouring itself
and children running blindfold
around and around
in avenues gray
among shadows of futures past

Oblivious to a portrait
captured in last light
sparkled upon the crimson horizon
and melting into shade
Their laughter

as light filling a void
where once was a presence
fading into time
in a glass darkly painted
this the final touch
of a self portrait

L. A. Espriux

WOOD SLEEPER

Sometime I am confused
In a wood when it is nearly dark--
Nearly I lose my way
Like an old man that has drunk too much wine--

But he is more foolish than I!
He doesn't realize the wind cold,
Nor that his feet will surely die
Because of cracks in his shoes;
He doesn't know that I
Watch him dance in circles
Around the holes of foxes until dawn...

Then someone else will come.
Will step clumsy through briar and shadow
Only to discover an old man propped pleasantly
Under a tree with an empty bottle in his hand.
And he will most certainly say:
How fortunate he is to sleep
With so much happiness in his mind!

...Sometime I like the snow
In a wood when it is nearly dark--
Nearly I am lead astray
By ghost that haunt the shadows--
By people and places that refuse
To stay buried beneath the snow--
By --and by--

But they are all dead now
All that generation a dream long ago;
All vanished as winter rabbits in snow

Sleep brave boys...
Sleep fair brothers...
Sleep lost lovers and
friends...

Sleep!

THE LAST STATUE

The hummingbird approaches soundless
on wings invisible
A thin melody of hope
stretched between earth and sky
She is the truth of beauty
dreamed by muses ashes now
Honeysuckle-born on wind
she hovers briefly over
a valley burning harvest rich
song of thunder far away

Statue of one not dead
concealed in time divided by time
Spirit swift as an arrow
piercing heart of alabaster
to roll back stones of lost memory
resurrecting dust of fallen centuries

A fluttering by chance
too near the marble brow
vexed with a crown of thorns
troubles the silence
with a memorial forever written
in ashes at his feet
This Hope Shall Endure

L. A. Espriux

DREAMER

I dreamed a dream
reborn with wings
My life reshaped hollow
by a peculiar lightness in my bones
So high above worldly cares
I ride the celestial winds
and dream yet another dream
And in this dream I hear
a sound like thunder
Voice of a boy given a new gun
laughing in the shadows below earth
and sky fading darkly
as I fall from on high
in my dream

L. A. Espriux

ADONIS OF THE NIGHT

Surrounded in night
All so pure and right
The moon as naked Adonis in flight His
shadow cotton fields
Blossomed with erotic dreams
His dream her dream
Entangled together lost together
Found together forever the moment The
moist reality of flesh on flesh
This their purpose clearly written
His purpose her purpose
Mingled in the dust of Adam with Eve
The desperate quest for immortality
In this solitary mortal moment
And in the brightness of morning
She asks was it love
Was she loved
Was she only whore
Of his dream

L.A. Espriux

Adam Born

Man alone
A new ocean burning
in his eyes with salt
with memories
he only vaguely feels
with acute emptiness
in distance of silence
pressed into darkness
of generations past

Visions of war
frozen in a pool of conscience
Faces pressed timeless in the sand
a face his own
a face he no longer knows
Emptiness of love
he no longer remembers
His heart cleaved in two
divided in the midst of sea
mingling his blood in the surf
His soul bled out

All history only dreams now
All ghost dissolving into ebb
of a distant universe
fading into new heaven
His spirit quickened a second time
born again
naked among stars

L. A. Espriux

MIRROR OF EVE

She looks in the mirror
across time and shades
immortal
Her mother's eyes
winter blue
somehow sad and empty
reflected in the illusion of glass
a promise of enmity and remorse
And all the jewels
and all the satins
given as gifts and pleasures
Hers now to inherit
reaching always to love
to be and never be
Her flesh made beauty
through eyes desired
to weave countless generations
mingled in her blood and soul
until husk of flesh changed
a cracked and darkened
reflection in this mirror beheld
Her tears dried up
as desert sand
slipping through delicate fingers
clutching distant memory
as when once
she too was young

L. A. Espriux

PATH FINDER

I am not afraid
of wild beast and shadows
Nor silences of lost nights
lost in a wilderness
A place of no man's land
in dark reflection of a new moon
that follows winter tracks
made in the sun

At times I imagine a jungle
rich and tangled beyond
the muzzle of snow-covered hills
Sometime naked trees are more human
Their flesh more subtle
than my weathered bark
At times I think the wind my father
My mother an ocean of dark clouds
These memories like new snow
so soon to melt
too soon forgotten

At times I watch in secret
a herd of restless spirits
as they claw the frozen earth
in search of peace
Then they see me and are gone
Only wind now to keep me company
Only emptiness to hide my shame
At times I fear I have lived too long
That I have become solitary without cause

That I have slain too many buffalo for warmth
And have rolled back darkness too many
only now to lose my own way

At times in the quiet of an hour
I wish to sleep at last
To feel my soul seep into cracks
made before this presence
separated purposefully in season
to hibernate until spring resurrection

I am tired oh God
Tired of the killing
Tired of millstones
Tired of hypocrites
Hear me oh God
Even in this dream
Wish of another path mortal
through time again

L. A. Espriux

THE NIGHT FATHER CAME HOME

The cigarette
red eye glowing dim
in the dark
Demon-eyed
when father came home drunk
tall and handsome like a huntsman
His eyes stained with too much wine
a visage pondered deeply
in the marred surface
of the dining table brought over after
the English woman died next door
Only to see
or think to see a reflection
twice reflected in his eyes
as dark as the table
His heart changed darker than the night
as he knows for the first time
a woman breathing in the shadows
Crouched against the wall beneath
shadow of a beast once a man
mixed with a presence from long ago
The dry bones of his father
buried in a pauper's grave
as a week later
the church closes its doors
and the cemetery infested with weeds
Still white flowers sprout year after year
above his head
like memories in a nearly dark hotel room
where last he made love

then died alone
always a gentleman to the last
He sees her naked
lying in his daughter's bed
The violence not altogether his own
Altogether could he never imagine alone
anything more beautiful
nothing more painful
than the unreality shuddering in his loins
Next morning
father drinks English tea as usual
the steam dripping from
his horn-rimmed glasses like tears
It is Sunday after Easter
and mother is gone early to church
to burn candles alone
And he never says a word to her
The silence
The horror
that has lasted even until now

L.A. Espriux

FOUNTAIN AT MYCENAE

Lethe has gone dry
And the fountain at Mycenae
Reminds the gods
Of their sweet nectar
Wasted upon proud civilization

Headless Eros
Naked and erect in the center
Bow straining against a broken arrow
His rust stained mouth
Sucking air

Ruins of an abandoned necropolis
In memory of fallen Olympus
And reaching across the court
Stands pitiful Aphrodite
Separate and alone
Mourning still the shame
Of a once cherished son

L. A. Espriux

THE DANCER

bronze feet
turning on hot pavement
rising and falling
faster and faster
brass coins
jingling
to the rhythm
of wine drunk musicians
laughing and smoking
intently watching
bare legs
descending
from the scarlet canopy
below a dancing girl's
twirling
silver belly button

gypsy madness
growing dim
in burning tired red eyes
of dying torches

L.A. Espriux

DREAM OF AN EMPEROR

Your eyes today
captured in a Tokyo
sunset splashed with
snow-capped mountains
centered in an onyx pool

A Japanese garden
surrounded in ebon centuries
transcending this moment
when I was an Emperor
in the days of Samurai
remembering your soul
woven into distant constellations
with last embers
of an oriental sunset
long ago

How soft your lips then
a last kiss before dark
now and forever goodbye

And I am reminded
of ghost in moon-lit night
and naked flesh shivering
pale in frozen light
before you became ashes
scattered by wind
in a valley rich
where once a tended garden

enshrined timeless
in this temple
of my heart

L. A. Espriux

ANCESTRAL MEMORIES

I wish to die in this climate
I say to my mama each time I come home
And stand at the feet of the Blue Ridge
Overlooking our house

What do you mean child
A little absence is sometimes good
Besides we all love you being here

She knows what I am talking about
Remembers all the seasons gone by
Since I first marched away
Silences blanketing the hills in autumn
The old buried and the young with children
A patio where the giant Sweet gum used to grow

It never seems that long ago
My little brother Rudy plays G.I. Joe
Younger Penny born with angel's hair
Pretending dress-up with her Barbie doll
And baby Cendi an unbound nature child
Running naked in winter snow

Mom prays often for a sign
Dad sometimes drinks too much
As he dreams of oceans over the mountain
A ship somewhere always waiting
Quick ticket to Borneo or India
Passage to exotic continents visited

Through adventure of a younger man
A time too long ago in his mind
So he drinks whiskey to forget
Then I go to war

Rudy quits school for a job at the cotton mill
Penny marries a mountain man
With a strong hand and hunting dogs
Cendi twice divorced back home again

We all weep at reunions
Laugh for all the old times
But never is it the same again
Never again so innocent
As when first I stand above rim of time
To watch shadows change
At the feet of the Blue Ridge
Overlooking our house

And say again to my mama
I wish to die in this climate

L. A. Espriux

Visions of the Old South

Old women sit
in old rocking chairs
that creak on old wooden porches
of mill village houses
built long ago.

Tapping padded feet
keep time
to the ticking-tock
of a Grandfather clock
from hand-me-down generations;

Heat quivering through cracks
in the new tar and gravel road
mixed with cotton thread and dye;

The air heavy
laden with chemical odor;
Spun into memories of buried husbands
and children that work graveyard
born prisoners from the womb.

In the worm-spittle
of cocoon-silk hair
evening sits and spins
webby nest
of tangled nightingale songs;

A fading melody
that sounds of laughter
escaping cracked withered
lips too tired to smile.

Too exhausted even to care
Now that another day gone.

L. A. Espriux

COMMON DESIRE

Pinter said
A leg is only a leg
A thing not more than you see
But if the thing you see
Is more than a leg
And if to see is to think to know
And to know is to be
And if all the world were to see
And to know and to be
And if Pinter right after all
That a leg is only a leg
Then what are you
To me

L. A. Espriux

TIME

In a shadow darkly seeing
Searching
But not believing
And through the soul
Like a specter
Precipitates this present

Past

To be is but mist
Thinly spread on window pane
Made flesh
Once changed
An ocean forever
Poured into time

Immutable

L. A. Espriux

WORDS

I have no words to express rolling
thunder in distant time as summer
rain falls between fl ashing plates
And how might I
or any one mortal describe the
magic of a mountain lake held in a
palm perfectly still

Cupped in a drop of evening
shinning wonderfully until morning
rich and warm
as light trapped benevolently
In the same hand
that has scooped the valleys
and pressed rocks immovable

What greatness of words
more than this
might I express

L. A. Espriux

THE RECORD

I trace the flesh
on back of my hand
much like lines on any map
texture here not so clear
as on the other side
the side that has handled
the hard earth of Adam's grave
the side that has touched
and been touched so softly
so clearly that still the memory lasts
as though yesterday
again today

On this side
at least
the record more true
lines crossing lines
obscured by generations
I have forgotten
and acts of violence
that should never be
forgotten

L. A. Espriux

CONVERSION

you gave him the best
years of your life
the marrow and the cup
your beauty and your soul

he was your cross
as you clung to him crying
Abba -Abba--
because of the pain

and I by your side
left to worship a greater love
greater than what we knew
that night in the temple
that night beneath
the silver Star of David
made of a vow
none able to keep

L. A. Espriux

EYES OF A CHILD

Through the eyes of
a child I see
Myself
as I may be
Innocent
Wise
Spirit free
If only through
the eye of a child
I might again be

L. A. Espriux

BEE QUEST

It is a honey bee
Lush of spring in morning air
Rises to meet the butter-cupped heads
Open mouths drinking
The amber coated light
As one by one pauses on each velvet lip
And with gentle soothing tongue
Licks the moist linen of crystal throats
Undressed in tender presence
Of love's banded seraphim
And so dilate the flowers ever so desiring

To hear whispered melody
Of nature's fertile song

Once a rare and beautiful flower
A wild Lilly growing in valley
Waiting thousands of generations
For Royal Jelly love to ascend
Preserved in the kiss of a honey bee

Youth dreamed once such love
As might melt winter sky
Surfing waves of billowed clouds
To pass through windows in heavens's heart
And squeeze tightly between inviting breast
rooted forever in summer fields of paradise

This only the dream of a child
To think grand Celeste might descend
Or else it was your dream of love

And I only a dreamer's dream
Dreaming of you

Dreams of love to find love
Promise more disappointment
desire than ripe fruit
After a worm smites the core
The sweated hide concealing
from hungry eyes
That the shell only an illusion
A sad thing of death

Death in the garden
Is a lovely vicious thing
It is the wasp sting
That penetrates guarded walls
Within a beehive mortality
Dream of young pretty girls in summer dress
Changing a young man's heart to cinder
As easily as the fire that did consume
Those fortified cities of old

It is only this dream of love in love
That splinters my reason to madness
Knowledge that in the end we know
Less than first we began

It is a honey bee

Limping in thick suckle air

Which cleaves my heart in two

As I continue through mystery

To sift through fading petals
Of generations revived by mortal touch

Only to find you again and again
My rare and beautiful flower
This love testament of greater promise

Not forgotten with each passing kiss

L. A. Espriux

THE HAT

A hat stolen by the wind
Made of straw and patience
And dreams left behind
In some faraway place
Dreams as true
As once were my own

A hat watched dancing near the sun
The wind walking stooped
Suddenly faltering like an old man
Who has journeyed already
Too far

A hat abandoned in twilight
Crowned richly with evening dew
A myriad of jeweled reflections
Igniting my way

And as shadows descend
I am convinced
That it is a special hat
Designed perfect for no one else

L. A. Espriux

House of a Friend

Come in wounded spirit
And lie here
Beside the fire of my side;
Place your burden
In the steadfastness of my heart;
And rest reassured
By the fortress of my confidence.

Wounded spirit
Put aside your armor
Against my walls of truth;
And share with me the bread
Of my blessing.

As final surrender
Wounded spirit
Allow your body to be bound
By these unfailing arms
Knotted strong with hope.

L.A. Espriux

CUPID'S STING

In this forest filled with light
Cupid's arrow flies true his aim
To blind both reason and the sight
Piercing her soul adorned in wedding white
With mortal wound of lie all is right

It is this sting of Cupid's name
Changes course of this game
Held by hand of reflected light
Striking love to darkest night
Confused in forest blinding bright

L. A. Espriux

THE BEGINNING...

I have no conception of tomorrow
No memory of yesterday
The present vague as when Lazarus
slumbered in his grave
I see many reflections of myself
From withering to birth
and now old again
Eyes shimmered in darkness
Winking from infinity
Visions many
Pure as starlight
Past and future funneled together
From creation to apocalypse
Singularity beginning and ending
ending and beginning
All in a moment
Forever now...

L.A. Espriux

Seasons Past

Time passes
Stone faces eroded
Into a broken collage

I knew you in spring
Your hands warm
Touching the cool of my palms
Making the sap
To rise thick into strong limbs
So much you knew to do then
So tenderly tended to my desire
As I blossom in love
With summer shadows
Descending naked over your beauty
And drink your tears
As the morning dew
Garnishing all flesh in season

But we both changed in winter
Like all other dreams
Planted in time still to know
Your hands too cold
To touch my soul anymore
My heart too much melted
Into seasons of
splintered cracks

L. A. Espriux

ANOTHER PARABLE

Jesus said love me
But am I Jesus
To ask you to wash my feet
With your tear-wet hair
Feeling your tongue
Squirm between my sweaty toes

Jesus wore sandals
His feet caked
With the dry hot dust
Of Abraham and Moses
I wear boots
My feet
White wrinkled fish
Wrapped in rotting leather

Jesus said love me
But am I Jesus

L. A. Espriux

THE VISITATION

As the bird in my window
you have come to reflect
something of myself:

Now quiet;
Now the earth drifts forever,
the meadows white,
the valleys open without shame,
as new snow falls like dream
to renew innocence in us all...

Yet something says
All is not right,
that the world somehow less perfect;
Something says
Beware of heart strings
and lights that flicker
in the night for no reason;

Then I am reminded
of a voice that heals,
a hand to smooth the wrinkle on my brow;
I remember how distant the ocean;
The mountains silent now;

I remember I am a fool
born altogether out of season;
Reborn naked in the eyes of God,
wise and eternal,
watching in shadow always near;

Now glad for this season,
glad for the passionless silence when
you are not here;
Glad for the memory of your eyes
that make me think poetry;
And for the chance to know you
tenderly even once;

Glad for the truth that we share;
For the silliness given to lovers
and sometime strangers;
And for all the happiness
we have known and shall never know

And most glad for the song of a bird:
Sinuous echo deep within my soul
that sings more than this...

L. A. Espriux

REAL PROGRESS

Real time
like real poetry
is just another way
of stating the obvious

Of course one
should always avoid
too many clichés
as when the box boy
dropped a whole bag
of Mrs. Mooney's groceries
breaking all the eggs
Or when the sweeper got fired
for stealing a pack of cigarettes
during his coffee break

And what better metaphor
than a poor sales clerk
laid-off after fifteen years
just to make space
for a better computer
This is real
progress

L. A. Espriux

CHIRON'S GATE

What of war and mutilated children
Does it mean anything in a city
Where groan of bridges and traffic jams
Drown out the cries of butchered millions
What of bombs that suck away the air
Smashing mountains to rubbled slush
What are towers of stone and mortar
To wind of terror swallowing city lights
Leaving a trail of night in twisted landscapes
Grotesque with skeletal remains of skyscrapers
Swaying imperceptible in times of perdition
Death and silence arranged on empty squares
Like a chessboard prepared ready for end game
Where the subway conductor neither smiles nor frowns
But stares blankly up into the cavernous layers
As he pilots ghosts through mountains of ash
Through a gate dark and opened wide
Becoming maze of blind alleys
Ending in belly of nowhere

L. A. Espriux

WITCH HUNT

A poet
is loved in flesh
by only a few
because few hearts true

A poet
sees all
but remains invisible
Has comprehended
but remains misunderstood

A poet
whispers war
prays for peace
has felt dying
of many suns

A poet
has known
darkness collapsing into darkness
while pondering the flickering
center of every spinning galaxy

A poet
written to a generation
in love letters and parables
mixed with potions made
from shadows of mortal night
as strong salve to heal
superstition

L.A. Espriux

WINTER SLEEP

in winter
they grow cold
spirit-white
inside ice-painted catacombs

the sun changed dark
in their eyes
shattered mountain-glass falling

snow rainbow-tinted butterfly
wings in the air
visions of what was
will be again
miracles waiting still to be
born again

L. A. Espriux

WEDDING VOW

Name the price of true happiness
Days and nights passed from then to now
From heart to heart until all hearts the same
Promise of lost love doomed to love again.

Except this exchange a contract signed!
All fair in love and war--
This love the cost of my war!

So soft the moment so deceptively real
This pleasure named in living
Souls purchased beneath a Zodiac sign
Feet that stumble on anvil of time
Nothing exchanged that can ever survive
Promise sure is that all must die.

Except this exchange a contract signed!
All fair in love and war--
This love the price of my war!

Reflected from illusion of a Judas reward
To all is vanity on whom they feast
Starving souls gorged on emptiness of lie
Swollen fat with starvation of pride.

Except--this exchange a contract signed!
All fair in love and war--
This love the cost of my war!

L. A. Espriux

FROZEN DREAM

I see you love
behind grove of cottonwood
where the moon walks alone
in vision long ago

I see you love
behind wolves crouched among
stars where cold wind blows
and long night hunts alone

I see you love
among ghosts dressed in shadow
here the sun no longer shines
in this frozen dream
I walk now alone

L. A. Espriux

SOMETHING GOOD MAY COME

Something good may come

From Viet Nam, from Belfast,
From Egypt-
From nations that cling together

On mountain crags;

Or appear like fireflies in valleys of the world--
But something good may come

Something good may come

To the starving children

In New York and Los Angeles;

To the slain and the murdered;

And to the monsters who feed

On the brave and the innocent--

But something good may come.

The world dies all around us

Like love in our bed;

And the moon shuffles past

Curtained windows drawn

to keep our anger secret.

You say I never cared much.

I say I care too much--

But something good may come.

And when there are no more words

In distant silence we hear:

Something good may come from this

That none may know in the now--

But something good may come.

L. A. Espriux

FLIGHT OF ICARUS

Mounted on wings as an eagle
I have traversed starry oceans
In uncharted dreams
Without notion to look down
And witness the ebb of generation tides
Erased on contour of dissolving shore
Nor behold splendor of great derelicts
Heaped in forgotten trenches of time
Or glimpse the profound meaning
Framed in cryptic architecture
Of astounding ancient tombs
Protruding from sand and bursting at the seams
With gaping grottoes overflowed by tarnished treasure
Burning to stubble souls ignited by mortal greed

Steadfast I behold the face of another
Reflected in orb of brilliance beyond
Preferring to remain blind to this moment
That I might see by faith believing innocence
In certain promise made of greater stuff
Than even these melting wings
Poised above casual human gaze

L.A. Espriux

FINAL DUEL

Lear raged at heaven
Like my father raged at me!

The fool my father,
Me my father's fool.
We knew each other then:
The end of genesis,
The beginning of apocalypse;
Back to back and face to face,
Knowing and never knowing;
We spit our curses
In duel fashion
Tempting the strength of blood-tie-
Cursing all strength in blood-tie!
Then I kill my father.
Zip open the earth
And stuff him deep-
Back into the grave before he is born-
Making sure nothing
Will ever grow there again!

Lear raged at heaven
Like my father raged at me-
But he will never rage again!

L. A. Espriux

SOMETHING LEFT UNSAID

I never said I love you
when our souls melted beside the fire
When I gave you all the strength I possess
and you to me the passion I lack
So I read poetry in your eyes
gentle words whispered in shadows
from a book you handed me bound in alabaster
that I might discover for myself
the wisdom of Kipling etched in your heart

Nor did I say I love you
even as your flesh gave meaning to mine
in promise of a child never born
Our hope everlasting just the same
mystically conceived in mortal passing
like the Rubaiyat of a song lost to wind

I wouldn't say I love you
when you called me your Russian grandfather reborn
or else descended from the slain blood of Persians
raised in the year of the dragon when a prophet
fell from above holding judgment in his hand
And with songs of genesis in his breast

I couldn't say I love you
even when desire faded from your dreams
Unable to quench dry places you suffered then
because of dryer stones in my heart
because of past destines neither able to change

consuming us both in lasting silence
as cinders melting into stars

Tonight there is a black cat
that sees patiently through the window
crouched at his place opposite the glass
watching a hummingbird unmoving
as it dances tauntingly near
And in a moment I share longing
to be beautiful and to have wings
Which makes me wonder why I never said
I love you

L. A. Espriux

THE PROMISE

In a reason far away
Voice in thunder!
Flash of day!
In the silence of an hour
Birth of wonder!
Breath in clay!

Then lived a dragon in the moon;
Then unicorns dreamed in the sea;
Then stood a shadow after noon;
Then an echo to hear him say:
Birth of wonder!
Breath in clay!

Then whispered wind in desert shade;
Then spirits gathered on golden cloud-
Then voice in thunder!
Flash of day!
Then miracle to hear him say:

In a reason far away
Voice in thunder!
Flash of day!
In the silence of an hour
Birth of wonder!
Breath in clay!

L. A. Espriux

Storm Break

Two bodies
divided in an eclipse
of a storm just beginning
the air moist and bestial
their naked silhouettes
shadowed against the wall

Flash of violence
that blinds destinies
thundering of words
to quiver the elements
then they pass instantly away

And through the silence of rain
we hear a child cry
from the next room
reminding us both
that once we loved
each other

L. A. Espriux

WILD HERD

a twig breaks
gentle
when the stampede comes
wild animals crazed
because of bull-lust in their heads
eyes white like the moon

too stupid to know
the tremble in their hoofs
nor butchery of earth
beneath unshod fury

L. A. Espriux

THUNDERSTORM OVER L. A.

and she appears briefly
covering the city at mid-day
her eyes fire-born swords drawn
her tears legions of whispers
streaked along soot covered windows

she is the latter rain
an illusion of false hope
given to blind men and the unwashed
lost between the cracks
in the fl ash of a shadow
surrounded by concrete and granite
in a city of fallen tears

L. A. Espriux

KNIFE

fear is a knife
to kill or be killed
to destroy
or destroy within

it is a knife with a long blade
that is true
a blade
with substance
without life of its own
made an instrument
to be used

and this is the reason
why it is deadly
in your hand

L. A. Espriux

MONSTER

I had a dream
That you were not yourself
That you had become a monster
To suck out my heart
I dreamed it
As I may have dreamed
A dirty movie or pages in a book
Seeing you naked and alone

Then I know
I no longer remember
You at all
The dream my own
And I am the monster

L. A. Espriux

THE TOUCH

the touch of a dream
like the press of lips
when no one there...

an image glimpsed only
fleeing into a shadow
wings spread full
for fear of being discovered
a phantom unseen...

for fear of memories
that haunt crevices in time
to gather stiffly
as a dry skeleton in my closet...

perhaps there are no ghost
in the sky at sunset
gold-breasted and tattered
flying blindly away...

perhaps she is a vision only
touching the empty places
buried secret inside my heart
and my tears changed dry wells
for all things forgotten...

L. A. Espriux

AND THIS TOO IS A GIFT

I remember it all
like a trail of tears
My soul changed to water
My life desolate and wasted
as I retrace the wildernesses
I have crossed-

And this too is a gift!

I remember the cruel prejudice
as though preserved in a glass darkly
Dreams dashed to pieces
Hope lost along the way
My innocence laid to waste
by pride and betrayal
and by treaties so easily broken--

And this too is a gift!

I have watched the heavens
to see one star to shine
brighter from all the rest
I have dug deep into the earth
to find one seed to bear fruit
The sun has risen and set
more than a thousand days
since last I remember
And each day my ghost
haunts the horizon in search of peace
for a generation born too late

A generation buried too soon-

And this too is a gift!

I have waxed in strength like the hills
So strong that my hands changed rigid
My eyes turned to granite
I have become as the short seasons
in every man's life
with wood-songs and poetry
my only companions
Becoming in time a strange myth
As a cold wind that blows-

And this too is a gift!

I have seen the spirits
of all things passing
all things now and yet to come
Seen fire that is Hell everlasting-
Been lifted up in Christ
at the Second Coming-
I have been wise as a fool
Have been to the wise a fool-

And this too is a gift!

I have this gift still to give
Forgotten memory in me to live
A voice heard from wilderness
echoed clear through mountain pass
above the perch where eagles nest
Words spoken in the name of peace
Crooked paths made to crooked feet

Promises broken to a noble dead chief
For as long as the grass shall grow
And the wind shall blow-

And this too is a gift!

L. A. Espriux

ALSO REMEMBER THE CHILDREN

Echo
Of children playing somewhere
In time
A reflection in my mind
A moment when I must remember
And ask questions
For us all

Why the wind from distant
Places where I have been
Places always near in my heart
Whispering lies that I once was young

Why so many faces
Abandoned in shadows
Faces I have desired and never desired
Faces that fill dark parlors
Like flowers to intoxicate my thoughts
As I watch from above
And see shadows gather in the sun

Why must I return along vacant avenues
Filled with ghostly laughter and dry pavement
Alive with the clatter of little feet
Near the edge of a night unsearchable
Darkness weaving slowly around
A children's game played at twilight

Around and around a generation sings
Red Rover--Red Rover--

The world is nearly over--
Times time's motion around

Their ashen bodies fading Into
an abyss of light
Fading like lost butterfly wings
Confused in the air
Their song also fading Fading
Fading away

And by tears
I am convinced
That once I was a man
After all

L. A. Espriux

A Saying

A saying that is past saying
etchings found
on cave walls once upon a time
describing places in the heart
worn nearly smooth
before searing of raw flesh
night vision round as the moon
the owl dark emperor of dream

A saying that is past saying
heard in a city blind to light
boys who find an old man
sleeping in an alley
and knife him for the fun of it
only later to weep emptiness

A saying that is past saying
love must die of truth to know love
deep in the shadowy darkness of love
beyond selfish hope of ever finding love
touched by another soul in love
found almost too late
In a saying

L. A. Espriux

THE LETTER

I read your letter
again this morning
fleshed with tender remembrance

time absent
since the morning we met
no more fear of vacant streets
or lights that shine from nowhere
only to dissolve into a misty basin
of a sea divided in time divided
the parted memory that was us

this letter abandoned in solitude
abandoned in the absence of an hour
not mine not yours alone
abandoned like whispers at twilight
trees shivering naked bare-shouldered
a place and a time ending forever
shading our memories with uncertainty
obscure as all promises made and broken

words now empty like ghost in the air
beautiful with metaphor and meaning
embedded in an eroded part of my heart
erased from thought long ago

L. A. Espriux

APOCALYPSE

Tapestry in heaven
measured in time
a billion years unknown
to weave shadow of destiny
through art and superstition
observed in ghostly reflection
to outlast shining principalities
some fallen to darkness
others prepared to greater glory

But in the Zodiac end
war in heaven must prevail
when eye of Capricorn blinded forever
at the feet of Taurus consumed in a nova
Where tail of Scorpio lashes-out
wounding fierce Leo in the head
and shattering the heart of Virgo
as she reaches shamefully to Aries

And the remaining constellations
watch on through mounting chaos
waiting their domino turn
in the Apocalypse

L. A. Espriux

BATTLEFIELD

Flashes of crimson
drip in shadowy night;
Thundering blasts
strangles demon light!

Violent blade of a sharp knife
Slashes the earth until she bleeds;
And in salted graves
Prophecy sews serpent seeds!

From deep wounds sprout four:
Conquest-Hate-Famine-and Death;
And in hour of approaching darkness
Rises Chimera of another self!

Beneath shadow of crushing feet
Kneel wailing mothers for children that sleep;
Then silence before earth shattering roar

All flesh is my enemy--*I am war!*

L.A. Espriux

TERROR

The fear of passion
Surrounds me
Like the cold filthy hands
Of a corpse
The numbing fingers
Forcing into my bowels
Violating my reason

Purple swollen lips
Suck strength from my will
Gorging itself
With pulp of my emotion
Paralyzing the mind
In gnash of clinched teeth

Lowering my soul to shame
With slime spittle
Not even time can cleanse
As my heart reaches out
For your love to save me

Before fear altogether strangles
This rabid desire for you

L. A. Espriux

Conscripted Soldier

To become one with the dead
One baptized in fire of a true warrior
Ceasing to think or reason
Made one with the machine

The machine greater than fear
Greater than love, or hate, or desire
The machine greater than flesh and blood
Existing as purity of purpose only
As dark instinct driving animal passion

Mortal touch now the feel of cold metal
A cold in the soul moist as dead clay
Humanity stripped naked from the earth
Burning stars proof of a universe ignited
Proof of power to subdue all enemies save one

From purest reason arises this dark angel
Fire and judgment in his hand
A destroyer of worlds without end
A machine without thought or conscience
Thunder and lightning blistered in red morning sky
Odor of smoke and sweet death in the air
This parable recited by all men of war
A cadence in memory to the fallen

"All lost who enter here
May the one know meaning
In acts of many sufferings!"

L. A. Espriux

Morning Hunt

promise of something new
dark hills in early morning
the sun just beginning to rise

earth valley rich
dreams of warmer days to
come birds in the air
returning south bearing seeds

in their mouth
promise of spring in the air
promise of eternity
of all things made right
true in the sight
of the hunter's gun

L. A. Espriux

NEW BEGINNING

Middle of October
A breath like summer
And I awaken suddenly
With a dream in my heart
Only to realize my bed empty
My life more empty without you

Hidden in the husk
Of night crickets sing
Melody of a lullaby
Heard long ago
A song nearly forgotten
In warmth of day's past
A song shared that last evening
Huddled together beneath
River of the Milky Way
Fed by wondrous stellar sky
And in this pleasant stream

I sleep again
By early morning
Old man
Indian Summer
Creeps slowly out of bed
Glory of mountains
A crown on his head
Shadow of winter on his back
The journey cut short
And thinks little of where

He might sleep

In the afternoon
I sweep dead cobwebs
From my bedroom window
Making me recall the vision
Of distant childhood memory
A nimble spider spinning
New threads through silver light
Her days already numbered
Without fear or anticipation
She considers not the future
Knowing by instinct
Tomorrow never sure
Before falling startled
To earth

Midday a honey bee
Lumbers outcast and alone
Struggling just to stay above ground
The grass yellow and brown
Not a single flower left to receive him
Then a finger of cool air
Touches frail wings ever so gently
And vanishes quickly
Into fuse of season
Without trace

At sunset I feel you clear at last
Your heart warm in a cold country
Your eyes as winter sky
Inspiring me more brave
Than reluctance of nature

In absence
I am ready at last
Now prepared to seize tomorrow

No longer to fear the cold
No longer wish a way of escape
Into distant solitudes
Of my own thoughts

Now no more poetry to write
No other song to sing more true
Than to become whole in your arms
Free to lose myself in your love
As this new beginning begins

L. A. Espriux

WEB OF ANOTHER MAN

One snared in shadows
His hour long silences since
His dreams now dreams of another
His soul left in a dungeon
To rot until the Second Coming
Without any reprieve of hope

Brother--sister--mother--father--
Wife--son--daughter--lover--
All that once could have been
All dream that can never be again

All woven in patterns of dark illusion
To poison his brain with strange ideas
Until his bones and sinew
Changed to powder in time irresistible

In sudden flash of light
He sees himself caught in web of moonlight
And attends the crawling moments
That by this sign
His final salvation near

L.A. Espriux

CARNAL FACT

They sell us fear-you know
They say we can't live without them
because the world's not a perfect place
They say it's better to survive
than to live because it's more safe

Maybe... Just maybe...
They are right!

Maybe the shades are better left down
Maybe the night is more pleasant watching T.V.
Maybe Jews, Negroes, and Mexicans all thieves
better shot on sight than left to chance
Maybe a world less true more beautiful
more in the image of what we can all believe
Maybe the Mercedes, the BMWs, and the Cadillac's
All new office buildings and shopping centers
more important than trees and gardens
or those lost in poor ghetto alleys...
Then maybe all the rats and whores
might just disappear in a dream
and no one need be responsible
No one need to care as long as
They make all the right decisions...

As long as...
They don't build any more ovens
in my backyard...

L. A. Espriux

PLEA FOR CLEMENCY

There is nothing more I can say
to vanish nightmares
of starving children
and bleach blood stains
out of my mind

There is nothing more I can say
to wash away the ghetto poor
lost in city streets
where rich men laugh soulless
awaiting in turn their hour

There is nothing more I can say
to heal corruption
in this world of change
or to turn hearts of men
to the Son of God
risen whole from his grave

And in distant silence
I hear women weeping
as though in the apartment next door
and the sound of my own voice
saying always
and always saying
there is nothing more I can say

L. A. Espriux

STUDY BREAK

It is not poetic
when the moon hangs
in smudgy air
tarnished yellow
shot-through with blood
like a pneumatic illness
beyond hope
of nature's cure

The night
heaves a percolated sigh
to perennial vision
imagined in darkness
and begins to rain cats and dogs
or is it
just the sound of rain

L. A. Espriux

CONVICTION

I will is strong
when I am alone

but I am weak
when others speak
like whispered reeds
blown by temptation's
passing feet

L. A. Espriux

DeJa Vu

Summer is a land indeed
to the very young...

See-through skirts floating ghostly

over hill and valley in a park

complete with laughing children

and dogs that bark

Watchful old sit
counting shadows in the sun
as they wait their turn

Bronze-skinned men with silver eyes

gaze up at the sky and wish for rain

or something more true than rain

something more mortal than sky

And you are beside me
hair burning as August
like remnant of warmer dreams
to forever haunt the seasons
ghostly remnant
of summer's end felt in the air

But this *Deja Vu*

too long ago to be in my life time

too long ago to remember

the softness on your lips

How soft then

your eyes...

L. A. Espriux

DESTINY

A wise man remembers
The tragedy in being young
In a country where old men
Sit in the shade and share a pipe
Legends and fantasies blowing from the stem
Twining richly with smoke and recollections

He weeps
When their graying faces are gone
Their pipes cold and black in his mind
He weeps because of destiny
Star-born from the elements
And mountains that shake
His voice the sound of thunder
Heaven and earth pass as vapor
Into shadows of his heart
Fading into destiny

L. A. Espriux

ANOTHER DROUGHT

Glacier-smooth
Mountains with black teeth
As silent canyons without eyes
Deserts as brilliant crystal
Vast and empty like the sea

And he pauses for a moment
Beneath the withered plumage
Of another dead olive tree
Remains silent and prays

L.A. Espriux

Something Forgotten

Once
almost I can remember
Once
that her flesh made perfect
in my mind like a statue
chiseled in alabaster stone
Once
I believed her special
Once
that we were special
Once
the sea and the moon reflected
on rippling shore at midnight
as I read from a book of poetry
until changing of the tide
Once
maybe the touch of something more
Once
maybe something happy then
Once
something made real in metaphor
Once
maybe there is something forgotten
Once
only now I no longer recall

L. A. Espriux

LatterRain

Metaphor
of approaching storm
as angel wings streaked white
on confetti of clouds
tattered beyond recognition

the sun
peeks through lattice
of green shadows
to revive earth
with a wink

L. A. Espriux

DEDICATION TO THE POET

Someone says:
Your poetry stinks!
So I pause
to sniff the air.

True I have forgotten
to wash the night before;
my teeth stained yellow
in the black-spotted mirror
of a public toilet.

I think that I may be dying
from a rot disease
picked-up from only I know where;
I imagine pulsing boils
rising under my skin
making my legs wet
with genital sweat.

Then I relieve my fears
into the acrid pit
of a urinal;
and continue to pollute
the clustered sewers
with my poetry.

L. A. Espriux

LIES YOU KNOW

You know writes the poet
words must remain isolated
to proclaim witness of meaning
found in truth scribbled on subway walls
during period of gathering darkness

You know writes the poet
greater the world we think to see
greater temptations to be false
by escaping into another lie
that death of the soul just another illusion
to fool an audience convinced already
there is no hand of God

You know writes the poet
easier it is to hide in weak pleasures hoping
present need salvation enough

Maybe heaven might understand

there are things more important now
than to hear voice of living witness
that even fools and hypocrites understand

You know writes the poet
more sure promises of false idols

that tarnish in tended gardens

beneath hosts of glittering stars
Greater the monsters
crouched beneath neon shadows
between mammoth sky scrappers
standing side by side along dark alleys
infested with rats and reprobate
hiding sins of murdered whores and children

stuffed into garbage cans
flashed on the evening news
just because they wanted love

You know writes the poet
This witness of a poem more true
reflection of a message that might have been
glimpsed in approaching brightness of time
before true testament of this rhyme

You know writes the poet
These words written from before
Always the dead buried from the living
And always the living buried in fear
Thank you Jesus I continue by faith alone
Thank you Jesus when all the lies finished
Lies made of lesser things than
You know writes the poet

L. A. Espriux

LIKE US...

Like a butterfly you are free...
Like a worm I am reborn...
Like something once lovely
that can never be...
Like a season
we will always mourn...

L. A. Espriux

LITTLE CLOWN

Little clown..little clown..
My little clown...
So sad her little eyes I remember..
So laughing my eyes I remember...

Little clown..little clown..
Before you I live a foolish dream..
After you I am the foolish dream...
My little clown...

Pray to little Jesus for me..
I pray to you little Jesus...
Little clown..little clown..
My little clown...
I am you and you me...

L. A. Espriux

ONE NIGHT COMPANION

Time in a glass for a moment reflected
tells the whole story of our lives
wings frozen in a blur
touched by the cold breath of winter
in a season shorter than winter
dark and promiseless
yellowed photographs tied with ribbon
tucked carefully away in the drawer
to keep away lingering silence

Solitudes vaguely remembered
in waking dream

A candle that flickers solemnly
on the floor between us
casting pictographs wingless on the wall
As on window pane frost etches in
moonlight
reflections of past lovers and friends
Reminder of present reality
that we too are shadows passing
touched only and then forgotten

L. A. Espriux

VISITOR

In a late hour of the night,
The house quiet and closed-up tight;
There tiptoes into her room
A creepy crawly thing from an old cartoon;
And squats in the middle of her bed
To whisper bad dreams inside her head.

And so it says:
Sometimes I'm funny like a laughing baboon;
Sometimes I am the grinning moon;
Sometimes I am something bad you read;
Sometimes the thing terrible you said!

And so she says:
In the dark you really look a fright-
Mommy please come help me to fight!

And so mommy says:
Cry not my baby mommy is here tonight;
Bad dreams run away always from light!

L. A. Espriux

READ THE END

There is wind

in barren places

There is violence

in graying faces

There is--

How can it be rightly read

A place

more tangled than Homer's head

more twisting than the river Styx

crookedly sewn in a witch's stitch

There is--

How should it be properly read

A place

where lovers lie in bed

where words forever flying

into night ever dying

There is wind

in barren places

There is violence
in graying faces--
How else might this end be read

L. A. Espriux

OF A WOMAN THAT I MET

I see a dove
Rising with the sun
Her bright wings pure against cobalt
As I imagine the veiled eyes

Of a woman that I met

She is not that bird
With delicate neck and shade of pastel
Fleshed in early morning light
Nor shall I forget the change of wind
That takes her silently away
Leaving me confused in memory

Of a woman that I met

In late afternoon I see a flower grow
Violet head swaying in and out of shadow
Sweat of sweet honey upon elegant throat
Air that drips warm nectar mixed
With rich perfumed fragrance lingering still

Of a woman that I met

She is not that flower
Surrounded in a soft green bed
Shadows that grow long through shorter days
And still her loveliness endures
Resurrected again and again in dream
Of my heart pressed into seasons past

Of a woman that I met

At twilight I witness stars born
A myriad enumerable burning over oceans deep
The moon shimmering beauty in their midst
Adorned in fine linen flowing into night
Steps elegant across dark velvet sky
A presence laced in special demure

Of a woman that I met

She is not subject to those distant suns
Still unchanging points of light
To navigate lost sailors and poets
Nor her beauty stuff of present regret
Spun from mortal web fertilely sewn
Made flesh and blood and hope
Of a woman that I met

L. A. Espriux

Time Thinker

In silence I sit
Write poetry
The trees naked outside my window
I sit and remember
Wounds that were deep
Wounds that never heal

Times like this I wonder
Am I a man or am I spirit
Is there sinew in my flesh
Like the snow-covered earth
My veins frozen rivers
Do my prayers make the north wind
And do the birds that light in my branches
Know that my heart made more than wood
More than a season forgotten

In the moonlight
I see a rabbit caught in a snare
Almost I am filled with compassion
Almost it should escape
But sadly I too must eat
And remain strong pretense of presence

In the morning I think
To cast bread to the birds
Made rich with my own blood
This I hope enough to ease my guilt
Enough sacrifice to the living

By noon I feel my mind
Slipping once more into a dream
A dream of war and youthful fear
A dream where the dead unable to rise
Where thought only timeless solitude
And waiting and forever waiting

It is time to awaken again
From this dream I know
All the world must in time
Awaken from dream I know
Dreams I have dreamed
All dreamed in time

L. A. Espriux

SHOOTINGSQUIRRELS

In the morning
In a forest barren of shadows
A boy sits on a throne of dead poppy leaves
His new pellet gun in hand
He sees himself proud in his father's eyes
In a vision with five fine pelts
Dangling bloody along his thigh
How richly adorned
Like an Indian when this world savage
An endless forest thick with trees
And hidden valleys bleeding many rivers
When all spoke a single language
Made of signs and wonders
That in his generation he might discover wisdom
His father inherited from his father
Imparting knowledge of life and death
So proudly reflected in the father's eyes

L. A. Espriux

THE OMEGA DREAM

The bell...the bell...
Echo of world's forgotten--
Now and forever lost!
Swallowed in a hungry vortex
Time divided by time of lying:
Gray hair fallen
From an old man's head slowly
Dying!

The bell...The bell...
Death eternal cries greater tears than life
Lost paradise divided by bloody knife--
I see in a dream another dream
A dream unlike any other seen.
In this dream there is a crow--
If a crow may be named a crow
With falcon beak and a prophet's
Soul!

The bell...The bell...
Sounds of mourning to graves below
As a new sun approaches from the east
Resting still upon a hill made of enmity;
Exhaling hot breath upon dying race
Cries of agony beneath shimmering face.
Gazes skyward into light deceived,
The fowl flaps shadowy wings;
And to orb of fading twilight sings
Of men and their passing inscribed on
Stone!

The bell...the bell...
Night changed instant to day!
Of things made right in time made wrong!
Sings he of wars captured in diplomat debate!
Peace lost in battles won too late!
Graves of the innocent marking future estate!
Metamorphosis of something better sewn
In more fertile fields than in this present
Known!

The Bell...the bell...
Darkness into darkness shadows fly
Windswept plains and desert sigh
Lost in memory those days before
Mothers barren their breasts withered dry
Where once a paradise forgotten--
Nevermore!

L. A. Espriux

To Paint a Poem

If I could paint a poem imperfect
Transform a desert beautiful as I see
Shower the clouds with pink angels
Undress the moon over a turquoise sea
Fill the night with bright tiger's eyes
Brazen the morning with golden hair

If I could swear by total devotion
Sew in heaven a covenant of jewels
Make lovely music in the tabernacle of souls
My life sipped from the same immortal cup

If I could change the course of mythical rivers
Unravel the shadows between every sunset
Weave again mysterious threads in abandoned webs
Preserve the moment of even one destiny

If this poem were a living testament new
Sent to illuminate earth as heaven
The distant stars spiritual reflection
Proclaiming birth of better creation
Then what words might paint more true
Than the glory plucked in a handful of flowers
So convincingly perfect that not even a poet
May capture their meaning of fleeing loveliness

L. A. Espriux

THE GLIMMERING

To glimpse a moment in her eyes
Of dark exotic wood in forgotten deeps
All that is truth all the lies
Satin nights warm with her sighs
Reflections deep where she sleeps
Dreams of youth that she keeps
Between her thighs his dream dreaming
Through her pure and forever being

And all the world seeming dreaming
Of things pure and forever gleaming
Forever fleeting in her eyes
Where nothing lives nothing dies
Broken angels cloaked in summer flies
Church doors open to the last
All stand veiled before the mast
And she a shadow on the wall
To those present and those past

All things fallen and all things to fall
All creation gathered at the last call
She a spirit in church bells ringing
In her heart lost souls singing
She the past of all remembering
A guiding star in distant glimmering

L. A. Espriux

CHINA EYES

Her eyes his mother's eyes
Painted on a china doll given by his father
Before his father passed on
Before the sun and the moon divided
By a tapestry of silver and of gold
Before an onyx pool filled the center
Of the room that she loved where he died
Her place of solitude and belonging
The silent hours into eternity
Her remaining existence slipping away
Into dark corners of past memories
When his son but an infant
Swaddled in the sleek oriental wood
Creviced in the ebony of her arms
Her eyes into his eyes born again
In the rich Eden of her thoughts
His shadow watching in a garden
Touching the shadow of her soul
Until all the world changed to shadow

And all shadows changed to light
Her eyes the eyes of a doll
His mother's eyes deep and nurturing
Reflected far away in a land invisible
Where he is still a child
Watching secretly the tears flow
From her painted eyes
So long ago

L. A. Espriux

EYES OF PHARAOH

Eyes reflected in the soul of Pharaoh
Deep and penetrating
Born of illusion and disappointment
As if light were wings to carry him
Across time and shadow when
Moses born an infant in slender princess arms
Reaching across bright constellations
The circumference of a new moon
Etched delicately among the stars
As a wind tip-toeing ever so softly
In still Arabian night filled with passions
With dreams and with hopes
Sparkled in the sand of things past
And of things that soon must be

He rises in noble countenance
A queen by his side to divide centuries
Beyond the River Nile
A scepter of purest gold in hand
In vision distant and translucent
As a lion hunched gloriously royal
Dreaming a land once young
In the eyes of an Egyptian king
That gaze into a zenith forever fixed
Reflected through mortal eyes

L. A. Espriux

MAN WITH NO LEGS

The man with no legs
comes in night after night
to watch the dancing girls
twirl around the *Silver Moon stage*
Like Humpty Dumpty
propped up on wooden stilts
his back against the wall
He laughs so loud that the wall shakes
his teeth white and gleaming
Inside a child still screaming
on a lonely Quebec train track
bloody mélange mingled with rain
strange reality that his legs
gone cut-off forever
and forever he will never again
dance with shadows in moon light
Never again run away free
to catch destiny of anymore trains

His eyes gleam
in shroud of darkness
just beyond the flashing stage lights
He leans precariously to one side
as though he might roll
from his careful perch
and break beneath those
lovely silver feet
But he does not
as though born
of more than wood and flesh
As though these dancers angels

sent on special mission to raise him up
at end of last performance

L.A. Espriux

Portrait of a woman being watched

Near a pool
Through ripple reflection of the moon
I watch you child woman
Nearly all alone woman

I see truth piercing deep
Sadness of things passed
Withered visions never again woman
Of a look never again the same
Never again his eyes

Never again the same desire
The touch of his lips only fading memory
Once whispering sighs of a young girl
Now forgotten in an emptiness
Filled by emptiness of love departed
A heart made stone in reflection
No longer you a child woman
In his eyes

And I remain a silhouette
Eclipsed to mortal vision
Once glimpsed by an artist's stroke
A shadow within shadow watching
Tangled in many lines
Of many lies

L. A. Espriux

ROOMS

In her mind
are rooms
made of gingham and calico
cats in the attic
china-girl tea cups and Russian eggs
painted palaces and frowning czars
even something her father
said would never last
stored safely in a cupboard
since before her mother grew gray
and forgotten

Rooms
built with silences and dreams
and special rooms known only to herself
entered at twilight
windowless
shadows on the wall
like visions of departed lovers and friends
ever present ghost
that continue to haunt places
obscure in her mind

L. A. Espriux

BORN AGAIN

I am born in Montreal
shimmering sensual sparkled in light
as a flower pushing through the snow
in early spring I am new
The years that were into years to be
And me in the middle

In twilight fading
I see distant countries in the sun
Warm pacific oceans that mingle my feet to sand
Santana Wind bronzing dead soil
As the parched soul of my father's land
When I once a man...
When I once a man...

That was my father's land
the dry earth his now and forever
That was my father's land
Before Cobras in the air and death
Swooping beautifully upon heads of innocence
Crimson falling from heaven like rain

I am a warrior then
Blood, sweat, and odor of Napalm
Jungles that never stop to weep
And to weep...
and to weep...
and to weep...

Blood in the air, in my eyes, in my mouth
The wail of children in night darker than night
Their cries lost in time slipped away as smoke
Left behind in green rich tapestry of that land
When I once a man ...
When I once a man...
Of my father's land...

L. A. Espriux

A New Poem of Flowers

Flowers
sprouting atop a mound
sad and lovely
Wind-swept
by changes in the air
signaling approach of frost

Time forever now
motion invisible unceasing
rich petals spread into the sun
as a vision to erase
thoughts mortal and weary
in my mind

Eyes closed tightly
I remain among the beautiful
making wish never to awaken
This poem new made flowers

L. A. Espriux

Counting Among the Sheep

You can never know a wolf
Until you have counted among the wolves
Sat at the council rock of the moon
Made laughter lost of reason soon
Stepped silent while shepherds sleep
As shadows counting among the sheep

You can never know a sheep
Until you have counted among the sheep
Surrendered love to the peace of night
Seen visions without eye of light
Unafraid to the sound of approaching feet
As wolves are counting among the sheep

L. A. Espriux

DANCING GIRL AT CABARET MADO

She dances on a thread of silver string
Moving spirited through breathless air
Suspended moment in celestial stream
A spotlight burning through shining hair

Her eyes the eclipse of constellations far
Orbiting the visage of a painted moon
As jewels forged in the heart of enchanted star
Lost in melody of a rock and roll tune

Her feet laced in sapphire and vermilion
Her shoes designed of shadow and light
They glimpse her presence in distant vision
Beneath burning suns cold in neon sky

All eyes watch but none really see
As she dances through their vacant eyes
An angel sent to set contrite spirits free
Releasing all from tangle of lies

I am this dancer reborn in elegant rhyme
Flashing apparition on stage of jasper and gold
A living poem recited beyond space and time
I watch as many come and many go

To gaze at the dancing girl of this place
Glimmer of hope reflected in their face
Glistened as ripe fruit hung on mortal vine
I dance their souls through empty space

Each Friday night at Cabaret Mado

L. A. Espriux

www.ingramcontent.com/pod-product-compliance
Lightning Source LLC
Chambersburg PA
CBHW051006140626
46546CB00016B/1002